Great Artists

Jackson Pollock

Joanne Mattern

ABDO
Publishing Company

JB
POLLOCK

visit us at
www.abdopub.com

Published by ABDO Publishing Company, 4940 Viking Drive, Edina, Minnesota 55435.
Copyright © 2005 by Abdo Consulting Group, Inc. International copyrights reserved in all
countries. No part of this book may be reproduced in any form without written permission
from the publisher. The Checkerboard Library™ is a trademark and logo of ABDO Publishing
Company.

Printed in the United States.

Cover Photo: Getty Images
Interior Photos: Art Resource pp. 11, 13, 17, 19, 20, 23, 25; Corbis pp. 9, 12, 15; Getty Images
    pp. 1, 5, 18, 21, 24, 27, 29

Series Coordinator: Megan Murphy
Editors: Megan M. Gunderson, Megan Murphy
Cover Design: Neil Klinepier
Interior Design: Dave Bullen

Library of Congress Cataloging-in-Publication Data

Mattern, Joanne, 1963-
    Jackson Pollock / Joanne Mattern.
        p. cm. -- (Great artists)
    Includes index.
    ISBN 1-59197-847-5
    1. Pollock, Jackson, 1912-1956--Juvenile literature. 2. Painters--United States--
Biography--Juvenile literature. I. Title.

ND237.P73M38 2005
759.13--dc22
[B]
                                                                    2004052809

Contents

Jackson Pollock

Jackson Pollock was a famous American painter. He was part of a movement called **Abstract** Expressionism. This type of art does not show realistic objects or people. Instead, it uses swirls of color and motion to show ideas or meaning.

Pollock did not paint the way artists usually do. He spread his **canvas** out on the floor. This way, he could paint on it from all four sides. Instead of using brushes to apply paint, he dripped the paint right on the canvas.

Pollock was very active when he worked. His paintings show a lot of movement and energy. This kind of art is called action painting. For this reason, Pollock's nickname was "Action Jackson."

Pollock was a great painter. He created many original masterpieces. But, his career was short-lived. Pollock died when he was only 44. However, he is considered one of the most important American artists.

Jackson Pollock

1912 ~ Jackson Pollock was born in Cody, Wyoming, on January 28.

1930 ~ Pollock moved with his brother Charles to New York City, New York.

1934 to 1935 ~ Pollock painted *Going West*.

1936 ~ Pollock worked through the WPA in a program that helped artists; he was introduced to artist David Siqueiros, who greatly influenced his work.

1945 ~ Pollock married Lee Krasner.

1947 ~ Pollock painted *Full Fathom Five*.

1948 and 1949 ~ *Life* magazine published articles about Pollock.

Early 1950s ~ Pollock painted the "Black Paintings." These works are very dark and angry.

1952 ~ Pollock painted *Convergence: Number 10, 1952*.

1956 ~ On August 11, Pollock was killed in a car accident.

Fun Facts

- Today, Jackson Pollock's Long Island home serves as the Pollock-Krasner House and Study Center.

- In 1947, Pollock was quoted as saying, "On the floor, I am more at ease. I feel nearer, more a part of the painting, since this way I can walk around in it, work from the four sides and be literally 'in the painting.'"

- Pollock earned several nicknames throughout his career. Among them were, "Action Jackson" and "The Drizzler."

- Pollock was born Paul Jackson Pollock. He dropped his first name when he started school at the Art Students League.

Early Years

Jackson Pollock was born in Cody, Wyoming, on January 28, 1912. His parents were LeRoy Pollock and Stella McClure Pollock. Jackson was the youngest of five boys. His brothers were Charles, Marvin, Frank, and Sanford.

The Pollock family did not live in Cody very long. When Jackson was only ten months old, his family moved to San Diego, California. In fact, the Pollocks moved many times during Jackson's childhood.

LeRoy Pollock was a farmer. He wanted his family to live well. But, he did not make much money farming. He was always looking for a better job. That is why the family moved so often.

Jackson's mother loved art. She encouraged Jackson and his brothers to paint. She even let them skip their chores if they were painting. Stella's encouragement made a strong impression on her children. All five grew up to work in the arts.

Growing up, Pollock and his brothers helped their father on farms and ranches in California and Arizona.

In Trouble

When he was young, Jackson got in a lot of trouble at school. He did not like to follow rules and often argued with his teachers. Jackson did not get along with his classmates either. In March 1928, Jackson was **expelled** from a school in Riverside, California, for arguing with a teacher.

A few months later, the Pollocks moved to Los Angeles. There, Jackson attended Manual Arts High School. He did not like this school either. Jackson and some of his friends wrote a paper **criticizing** other students. When the teachers caught Jackson handing out the paper, they expelled him.

Jackson got another chance to go to Manual Arts High School in September. He began taking art classes. In one class, he molded people and objects out of clay. His teacher encouraged him. But, Jackson did not think his work was good enough.

Soon, Jackson got into another fight. He punched a teacher this time. So, he was expelled again. His art teacher asked the

school to let him come back. Jackson was allowed to come to school in the morning to take art classes. However, he never graduated from high school.

Jackson realized he wanted to be an artist. But, he was not sure what kind of artist he should be. Even though he loved art, he was not sure he was any good at it. However, he would soon have a wonderful opportunity to study art.

As a young man, Pollock wore his hair long and dressed in funny clothes to get attention. He saw himself as different. This darkly colored self-portrait was created between 1930 and 1933.

Thomas Benton

At that same time, Jackson's brother Charles was living in New York City. He was studying at the Art Students League. His teacher was a famous artist named Thomas Hart Benton. Benton painted large **murals**.

Charles came home to Los Angeles for a visit during the summer of 1930. He told Jackson all about Benton and his art classes. Charles told Jackson he should come back to New York with him. Jackson agreed. That fall, the two brothers drove to New York City.

There, Jackson began studying under Benton at the Art Students League. Benton painted many murals showing scenes of American life. Jackson worked on some of Benton's murals. He posed for paintings, mixed paints, and cleaned the studio.

Thomas Hart Benton

Going West imitates Benton's "American scene" theme. Much of Pollock's early work focused on landscapes and figurative scenes.

One of Jackson's first paintings followed Benton's example. It is called *Going West*, and it was painted in 1934 and 1935. Like much of Jackson's early work, the image looks rough and **amateurish**. However, it is full of movement.

The WPA

Pollock had trouble drawing realistic scenes. He often felt frustrated because he could not make his art look the way he wanted it to. But, Benton and other teachers at the school continued to work with him. They felt Pollock's work was very emotional. And, they liked the energy in his art.

During this time, the United States was in the middle of the **Great Depression**. It was hard to find work and earn a living. Pollock only worked part-time. He felt it was more important to paint than to have a job.

In 1936, Pollock got lucky. He was accepted into a program run by the Works Progress Administration (WPA). The WPA was a government agency that paid artists, writers, and other people to perform jobs that benefited the public.

Pollock's job was to create a painting every four to eight weeks. These paintings would be hung in public buildings, such as post offices. He could choose any subject he wanted.

Now Pollock was a professional painter. Working with the WPA also introduced him to other artists. Pollock had found a group of people he liked being with. He felt like he was part of an important time in American art.

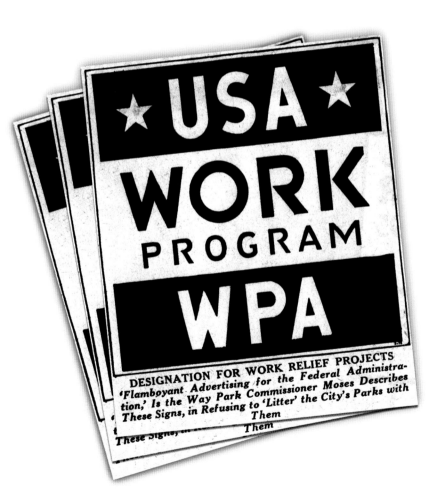

For his work with the WPA, Pollock earned about $91.50 a month. He worked for the program until it ended in 1943.

Artistic Ideas

Pollock spent a lot of time looking at paintings made by other artists. Many times, these paintings gave him ideas for his own work. The same year Pollock began working for the WPA, he joined a workshop taught by David Siqueiros. Siqueiros was a **mural** painter from Mexico.

Pollock had never seen anyone paint the way Siqueiros and his friends did. They mixed different kinds of paint together. Instead of using brushes, they poured or sprayed the paint onto **canvases**. They even painted with chocolate syrup! Pollock loved this style of painting.

Pollock also visited art museums and galleries. He enjoyed the work of artists such as José Orozco and Pablo Picasso. These artists used shapes and symbols to express ideas. Pollock began to use this **technique** in his own work. His new paintings began to look very different.

Artist's Corner

Jackson Pollock

Abstract Expressionism was an artistic trend in the early 1900s. There were many different styles. Typically, the artist tried to convey an idea or emotion without using recognizable shapes. The artist worked more with color and the way paint was applied to the canvas.

Some artists used their hands. Others painted objects onto the canvas. Pollock was known for his style of action painting. He used sweeping, forceful brushstrokes and would often drip or pour paint directly onto the canvas.

In this painting by Pollock called *Flame*, the idea of a fire is evoked by the heavy, deliberate brushstrokes in red and yellow. There is no concrete image of a fire in this painting, yet viewers think of a fire when they look at it.

Two Women

During the early 1940s, Pollock met two women who would be very important in his life. The first was an artist named Lee Krasner. Pollock met Krasner when they were both invited to be part of a show at a New York gallery.

Krasner knew most of the artists in New York, but she did not know Pollock. So, she went to his studio to see his work. Krasner was surprised and excited when she saw Pollock's paintings.

Krasner and Pollock married in 1945. They moved to an old farmhouse near the water on Long Island in New York State. The house had plenty of room for both artists to have studios. It was a quiet and inspiring place to work.

Lee Krasner in 1953

The She-Wolf *was completed in 1943. Pollock's exposure to Abstract Expressionism helped him realize he didn't have to draw realistic pictures to make art.*

During this time, Pollock also worked with a woman named Peggy Guggenheim. Guggenheim came from a very rich family. She loved art and collected a lot of paintings.

Guggenheim showed Pollock's paintings at her gallery in New York City. She also lent Pollock money and arranged for him to have his own art show. Because of Guggenheim's help, Pollock was able to support himself as a painter.

New Kind of Art

Pollock set up his studio in a barn at his house on Long Island. Here, he began to create a whole new kind of artwork.

Instead of putting his **canvas** on an **easel**, Pollock spread it out on the floor. He did not use brushes or art paint either. Instead, Pollock worked with the kind of paint used for houses and businesses.

Pollock began using the drip-and-splash method he would become best known for. He poured and dripped the paint right onto the canvas. Sometimes, he spread the paint around with sticks, **trowels**, or even knives.

In 1947, Pollock painted *Full Fathom Five*. In this painting, he covered the canvas with thick swirls and lines of paint. Then he added ordinary objects like nails, buttons, keys, and pebbles.

Full Fathom Five

Pollock had finally found the kind of art he wanted to make. His pictures did not show realistic objects. Instead, they were a design of loops, lines, and swirls. Pollock worked on a painting from all sides. This made him feel like he was part of the painting.

Pollock's paintings are full of motion and energy. Some people thought the pictures looked like someone just threw paint on the **canvas**. But, Pollock had a plan for each picture. He knew exactly what he wanted to create and how to create it.

Pollock also used a mixture of sand and broken glass to add texture to his paintings.

Fame

Soon, more people began to hear about Pollock's **unique** style of painting. In 1948 and 1949, *Life* magazine published articles about Pollock. The 1949 article was called "Jackson Pollock: Is He the Greatest Living Painter in the United States?"

Unfortunately, the writer did not really understand Pollock and **criticized** his **technique**. In 1950, *Time* magazine also wrote about Pollock's work. Again, the writer did not understand him. The article made fun of Pollock's style and suggested he was not a real artist.

The *Life* and *Time* articles introduced Pollock to people all over America. Many people came to see his shows in New York. But, most still did not understand Pollock's style of painting.

One of Pollock's unusual practices was to get a brush full of paint and let it dry. Then, he used the same brush to sling wet paint onto a canvas.

Anger

Pollock acted like he did not care what people thought of him. He tried to ignore what they said. But, he was angry that people did not understand his style of painting.

Pollock had never been a happy person. Now, he became even more sad and angry. He began to drink too much alcohol. During a party, he overturned a table full of food onto his guests.

Pollock continued to paint during this difficult time. The pictures he made during the early 1950s are called the "Black Paintings." They are darker and more violent than his earlier work. They use a lot of black lines and blobs. Some of the pictures include twisted and distorted faces.

Pollock spent much of his time painting in his studio. Today, his studio is part of the Pollock-Krasner House and Study Center.

Paint by Number

Pollock often numbered his paintings instead of giving them names. In an interview with The New Yorker *magazine, Pollock and Krasner explained that giving a title to a painting could make people expect to see certain images in it. Numbers have less meaning. For this reason, Pollock numbered his pictures so people would "look at a picture for what it is—pure painting." Pollock also said he wanted his paintings to challenge his audience and make them think.*

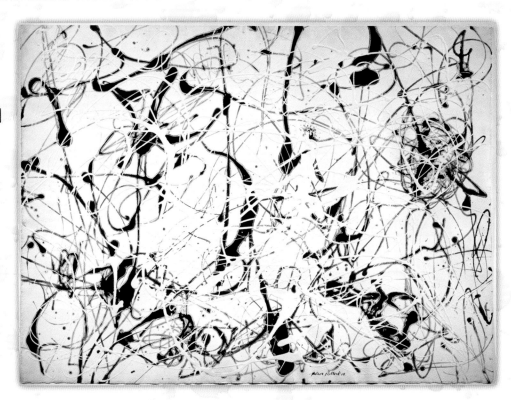

Number 23

Dying Young

Despite his hardships, Pollock continued to paint. He did not produce as many works as he had in earlier years. But, he continued to experiment with his **technique**. During this time, many of his paintings were done in layers.

One of these paintings was *Convergence: Number 10, 1952*. To create this painting, Pollock squirted paint right out of the tubes to add colors over a black-and-white background. The finished painting is full of tension and energy.

Pollock continued to have dark and angry moods. He eventually stopped painting altogether. Also, Pollock and Krasner were not getting along. Krasner decided to get away for a while. So, she went to Europe without Pollock to work on her art.

On August 11, 1956, Pollock drank too much alcohol at a party. Then, he got in his car to drive home. Pollock drove too fast and lost control on a curve. The car crashed into some trees, and Pollock was killed instantly. He was only 44 years old.

Pollock's headstone is in the Green River Cemetery in Springs, New York. Pollock and Krasner lived in Springs for about 10 years. The city was considered the artistic heart of the Hamptons, a neighborhood on the eastern end of Long Island, New York.

JANUARY 28, 1912 – AUGUST 11, 1956

Many people thought Pollock's death was symbolic of the violence he had shown in his work. But, the car crash was simply a tragic accident. His passing robbed the art world of one of its most exciting young painters.

His Legacy

While he was alive, Pollock did not sell many of his paintings. Most people were more interested in his wild life and **unique** style. They did not understand what he was trying to say through his art.

After his death, art critics began to understand and appreciate Pollock's work. His style has inspired many **abstract** painters. Today, he is considered to be one of the most **innovative** American artists.

Pollock produced many paintings during his short career. Now, these paintings hang in famous museums. They can be seen in the Museum of Modern Art in New York City, the Tate Collection galleries in the United Kingdom, and the Smithsonian American Art Museum in Washington, D.C.

A woman looks at Pollock's One (Number 31, 1950) at the Museum of Modern Art. Pirate by Willem de Kooning is seen on the left.

Glossary

abstract - relating to something that doesn't represent a real object but expresses ideas or emotions.

amateur - a person who does not have a lot of experience in a certain field.

canvas - a piece of cloth that is framed and used as a surface for a painting.

criticize - to find fault with something.

easel - a stand that holds a painter's canvas.

expel - to force out.

Great Depression - a period (from 1929 to 1942) of worldwide economic trouble when there was little buying or selling, and many people could not find work.

innovative - something new, original, or unknown.

mural - a picture painted on a wall or ceiling.

technique - a method or style in which something is done.

trowel - a hand tool used for gardening, similar to a small shovel.

unique - being the only one of its kind.

Saying It

Guggenheim - GUG-uhn-heym
Krasner - KRAZ-nuhr
Orozco - oh-ROHS-koh
Picasso - pee-KAHS-oh
Pollock - PAHL-uhk
Siqueiros - see-KAY-rohs

Web Sites

To learn more about Jackson Pollock, visit ABDO Publishing Company on the World Wide Web at **www.abdopub.com**. Web sites about Pollock are featured on our Book Links page. These links are routinely monitored and updated to provide the most current information available.

Index